Letters from the Other Side of Haiti:
A Long Way Down

Jillayna Adamson

Libri Agni

Indianapolis   *Evansville*   *Chicago*

Libri Agni

Published in the United States by Libri Agni, an imprint of Bird Brain Publishing, a division of Bird Brain Productions, LLC, Evansville, Indiana. www.birdbrainpublishing.com

PRINTED IN THE UNITED STATES OF AMERICA

Photography by Jillayna Adamson
Cover design and graphic art by Whitney Arvin

First Edition
ISBN-10: 1937668800
ISBN-13: 978-1-937668-80-8

To all the incredible children I have come to know and love across Haiti. May you come to understand someday that there is a world full of people out there who love you, believe in you, and continue to root for you. I am just one of them.

Edeline, Wisly, Jezebelle, Bela, Sabine, and Medline, wherever you are.

In loving memory of Amy.
May we always know your heartfelt enthusiasm.

Prologue

"Its kinda funny, isn't it," my brother said, as we trudged down a rocky dirt road into the town of Pignon, "we're less than two hours from Miami, and people are riding donkeys and have no electricity or running water."

My older brother, a geomorphologist and hydrologist, does work for Haiti Outreach, a non-for-profit organization that focuses on clean water sources and is based out of Pignon, Haiti. Pignon is about 80 miles from Port Au Prince. I had been waiting to graduate from university to finally get the chance to come down. Working in third world countries had long been a dream of mine and Haiti was on my radar. After my fiancé and I graduated from university, (I, in psychology and anthropology with additional interests in writing and photography and child-youth across cultures; Rod, with a degree in Electrical Engineering) we raised money and set up a trip to do volunteer work and experience life in Pignon for one month.

We were finally there.

Thanks

Haiti Bound; Before take-off.

First of all, we really want to thank everyone who donated money, and other things for our trip to Haiti. Just within our close-circle of awesome family and friends, we raised about $1000 (plus supplies), which is definitely not easy in today's financial world. We are entirely grateful, and we know the people of Pignon and the Nene family (a local family we will be staying with) will be as well.

We bought (and been given) tons of coloring books, crayons, French and English children's books, toys, games, puzzles, sanitizers, first aid material, stuffed animals, underwear, soccer and play balls, dolls, gathering bags, water bottles, tons of child and adult clothes...We also have lots of 'candy cane mice' made for a charity by grade two students from Parkway Elementary, which we are bringing. And man oh man, there is a lot more.

As we all know, kids really need to play. We have gone out of our way to stock up on toys and learning tools for the Nene family, as well as kids in orphanage and school. We also have some helpful donations for the hospital. We will likely buy a few more necessities for the community once we are there, and plan to put the remaining raised money into a fund for the Nene kids' education. Endless thanks!!

My grandparents, Karen and Tom, Kendra and Brian and kids, Rod's family--special Thanks to Ruth, Naomi and Steve, Kathleen, Mike Diamond, David Schwartz, my parents, Angela and Cory, James and Amy, Emily, Allison, and all our other supporters!!

Lots of love!
Jillayna and Rod

LETTERS HOME

1-8-11

We Made it

We made it into Pignon yesterday, and thus far
have seen the town, as well as Port Au Prince. Port
Au Prince was expectedly hectic. As we walked to
meet our "cab", crowds of kids stood with their faces
mashed into the gates outside the airport, shouting at us. Many of them had missing limbs or were
somehow disfigured and were eagerly begging for
"one dollar". Eventually, pushing past clobbers of
Haitians grabbing at us and shouting in Creole and
botched English, we made it to our cab to the next
airport. This "cab" ride consisted of half of a rusty
car and a drunken Haitian man missing most of his
teeth and many fingers. He kept one (almost finger-
less) hand on the wheel and the other held a warm
Prestige beer. Kids hung onto the side of the car, and

he swerved often to try and knock them off. Rod and I watched their faces as they shouted to us, gripping white-knuckled at the windowpane.

At the next tiny airport-- which was a simple run-down building and a strip of grass-- we were all weighed and seated accordingly to balance our tiny plane out; Being the lightest, I was strapped into the back with the luggage. It was the type of tiny plane ride one could compare to a rollercoaster, where you feel every movement in the pit of your stomach. The views were nothing short of breath-taking. I watched the endless spread of mountain scenery and tiny clusters of huts and shacks, trying to ignore the thick drips of dark oil dripping from the plane's wing outside my window.
After 45 minutes, we had made it to the town of Pignon.

In Pignon, we have attracted many stares and much attention. It is quite strange being such an obvious minority. The kids are wide-eyed, playful and curious. They touch my face and hair, try on my sunglasses and call Rod and I "Blanc" (which means white in Creole).

The house mom we are staying with is very young and tiny...I would guess her to be in her early twenties. Her children are adorable and are constantly watching us. We gave her some presents including soaps, hair bands, a bag, fans, a sewing kit and some clothes. We also gave the kids a few toys, and they have been excited about their new 'noir' princess Barbie doll, crayons, coloring books, and balls to play with.

After meeting many people of the Haiti Outreach organization, we walked around Pignon gathering stares, but always with polite a "bonjou". We quickly learned that a smile and greeting brings a happy, friendly reply.

Goats, chickens and horribly thin dogs wander the dirt roads. Girls walk effortlessly balancing jugs of water or baskets on their heads. Some people ride donkeys, and there are also a few motor bikes. Straw and mud huts line the streets, as well as some tiny, wildly painted pink and green stone homes. Some people sit outside selling goods, talking and braiding hair. The little kids wander around with dirty faces, either naked or without pants. They are all gorgeous.

We walked a few miles down a dirt road to the weekly market. It was loud, crowded, absolute chaos, and very hot. Shoeless kids followed us, tugging at our shirts and arms. They asked me to take their pictures or hold their hands. Everyone wanted the "blancs" to come see their goods.

This place is beautiful and I think we are both already entirely in love.

Jillayna Adamson

Key Players

Celione (Sell-lee-own)- Our house mom, very young and very petite. She is sweet and always smiling. Her husband (who worked for Haiti Outreach) was killed after the earthquake, and Haiti Outreach built
her a house and gave her a job as a cook.

Medeline (Med-Leen)- The super-child 12 year old. Incredibly sweet
and very smart.

Sabine- 8. Very helpful, very giggly. (pictured Sabine and Gamonell)

Bela (Bay-la)- 4. A little stinker, but I'm absolutely in love with her. Always only in her underwear.

Gamonell (Gam-own-yell)- 2 or 3. Very cute. Always dirty.

Kiki - 5. A little clown

Cee - Baby. Obviously adorable. Always dirty. Eats a lot of dirt.

Dzioli (Zee-oh-lee) - Perhaps 16, male. A cousin who mostly lives there and helps out with more "manly" duties, like carving. Brings us sik can (sugar cane) to chew.

Viatrice - Male, in his 30's, born in Pignon, works for Haiti outreach. Takes us and drops us off on a 4-wheeler at different schools and does initial translating. Super helpful, speaks great English.

Donald (Do-nAl) - Instant friend, still in high school, born in Pignon and hired by the UN to translate. Helps us meet a lot of cool people.

Woudlin - From Pignon, about our age, and studying medicine in Port Au Prince. Made us carved beautiful necklaces and has a gorgeous family, also speaks pretty good English.

Katia - Woudlin's cousin. Also our age, has one young daughter and is anxious to learn English. Already doing quite well.

Wizner (Wis-ner) - From Pignon, is handicapped (Cerebral palsy), in his 30's, and works at the Campbell orphanage. Speaks amazing English and has been incredibly kind.

Jennifer and Bill Campbell - Run one of the only credible orphanages in Pignon, where we would spend a bit of time.

Edeline - A little 6 year old girl brought to the feeding clinic extremely malnourished, whom we would quickly fall in love with.

Wisly - A 15 year old orphan at the Campbell's orphanage who is incredibly smart, kind and driven. He speaks amazing English and took us on a hike up Mount Pignon.

1-10-11

Life in Haiti

The days have been consistently steaming hot and bright. That being said, we are always sweaty, caked in dirt, and I'm quite sure we smell by now (though bathing has been attempted). We are also constantly thirsty. We have experienced a whole lot in the last few days. While Pignon is a very calm, slow-paced village, we are still bombarded with all that is going on around us. Of course, the language barrier adds to that chaos, but we are picking it up quite well.

Our house mom (Celione) took us to a Haitian church service with her family. We were trying to figure out what it was she was trying to say to us as she waved her arms back and forth like windshield wipers. Dancing? Music? We couldn't get it. Then, one of the little kids (Sabine, 8, gorgeous) said "Jee-zize!" It took a couple minutes of saying it aloud to realize what she was saying...Jesus!

So, we walked (quite a long walk, I must add... They walk or take donkeys everywhere) with the family to their church. Tons of Haitians were walking with us down the dirt roads, alarmingly well-dressed in their whitest of whites. It was explained to me that they always save their absolute best for church. We piled into the pews, everyone sweaty and elbow to elbow (of course, we were hard to miss, and drew much commotion).

They are perhaps the most animated and spiritual people I have ever witnessed. As they pray, they all lean their heads back, close their eyes and wave their hands back and forth (the windshield wiper motion that Celione had been doing earlier). They sang a lot, in Creole, of course, and screamed out many "Hallelujas" and "Amen". And I do mean screamed. Rod stood and introduced us in Creole to the entire church, and afterwards when we shook hands with neighbors, people "blessed" us for visiting and said they would pray for us. A tiny girl, who was seated in front of us, sat backwards watching us for the entire service, smiling wildly and repeating "blanc blanc blanc!!"

For meals, we have mostly been eating rice and beans (pwa ak diri) cooked by a big Haitian woman in a little stick hut. I have been opting out of eating meat, but not surprisingly, Rod has been loving it. The food looks intimidating-- heaping piles of brown goo and rice. But it's actually quite good.

Thus far, we have actually enjoyed quite a few un-Haitian-like luxuries. For instance, to our surprise, we have a "room" in the widow's house. It even has a little bed. Of course, there is still no running water or electricity, and we do live amongst ginormous, glowing-eyed spiders, cockroaches, and tiny mice. The nights are dark, hot and sweaty. Some nights I have to soak my clothes to get to sleep. And I check my shoes every morning.

I have now mastered squatting. Our "bathroom" latrine is in the back-- it is simply a few buckets behind a stone wall. However, we sometimes use the bathrooms and the Haiti Outreach house--THAT'S a treat. Though it almost feels like an unfair luxury not available to the community—cheating, perhaps.

We have played endlessly with the kids, from soccer (footbal), a version of volleyball, simple magic tricks and hand games, and general goofing around. It is amazing how universal hand-clapping songs are. I actually knew a few (albeit in English) from my own elementary school days. We've been bringing out books and helping our family with English and they've been helping us with Creole. They are all such characters, and we've quickly gotten to know their personalities without always knowing what they're saying. They walk around gnawing on hunks of bread and love to come running out of the sugar cane fields with stalks in their mouths and juice running down their chins. It's quite a treat.

The eldest daughter of our family is 12. She takes care of all the younger ones. She's sweet, smart and very mature for her age. She really is just a little mother. She goes to the wells and hauls back water buckets (on her head of course) for the family, does laundry and cooks food. She carries most responsibility. The kids here all take care of younger kids, no complaints, worries or questions asked.

By the time the sun sets, we are entirely exhausted. We walk many miles every day. Interestingly, Haitians walk very slowly, showing little signs of hurry. At first, I was taken aback by it, and impatient. I walk much faster. But I have learned to slow my pace and walk in a more leisurely manner with them. They are rarely frazzled or stressed. They are never late. Mainly because there is no "late", no planner, no schedule, and they don't need to keep obsessive track of time. It is merely jour, swa or nwi (morning, afternoon, or night). They stop and talk to everyone. People are happy to sit outside their huts and talk and drink warm beer. They sing as they work. Everyone knows everyone and many of the people we meet actually turn out to be cousins.

We had a great day and pleasant evening with the family. We were invited to some kind of service vigil for Celione's deceased husband. It took place in their home and about fifteen people came. It was beautiful. We sat in a circle in the small stone room surrounding a candle lamp and an elderly, deep-voiced man who led us in prayers and songs. The wind was blowing and the curtains that go over every door and window blew in, swaying around us. It was dark, but we could make out expressions, emotional in prayer. We didn't even need to know most of what was being said to understand what was going on. The faces of love and loss transcend quite universally.

The four year old sat on my lap and clapped her hands when songs began. She fell asleep with her hands on mine and her head on my chest.

We also visited an orphanage today...such was difficult and relaying the experience must be saved for another time. Tomorrow we are going to do some work at a school. There is much to talk about, but we must retire for the night. We are loving every minute.

1-12-11

Jillayna Adamson

Jillayna Adamson

Rod helping dig for the well drilling

The Drilling truck

Our new friend Donald works as a translator for the UN base in Pignon. He took us to have coffee with the UN Captain stationed here.

Medeline, the 12 year old, cooking in their kitchen

Teaching English at the secondary school.

Visiting the Orphanage

Our food...pwa ak diri!

Rod trying to help fix a chlorinator

Jillayna Adamson

1-12-11

Orphanages and Teaching English

The Orphanage.

The other day we went to visit some children at an orphanage in Pignon. We are aware that this orphanage is not so properly run, and is corrupt. Let's just say that the orphanage owner's own biological children all sit in a nice, cool house with electricity, a satellite dish and laptops, and 62 orphans ranging from 3 to about 17 are outside working. I don't want to talk too much about the issues known about the orphanage now, rather, I will talk about the children.

One of the orphans, I'd guess his age to be perhaps 12, is severely disabled and in a wheelchair. He mostly sits alone on the porch with a huge, toothy smile and he loves attention--of which I'm sure he gets little. I couldn't help but wonder how long he sits out there in the heat with no pants or underwear.

Many of the kids were in their underwear washing the bus that takes them to school (Such is the good news, the kids DO get to go to school). The kids, all small, some quite young and scrawny, took turns pumping water from the well and carrying buckets to splash on the bus. They scrubbed, inside and out, showed us their tiny muscles, and were quite playful. Of course, it was all heartbreaking, but nice to play with the kids. While the orphanage is clearly corrupt, as so many are in Haiti, the kids are still kids that need love and support and have no control over their situation. We won't be donating money (lord knows what happens with it), but we will be back to play and visit.

Yesterday, we went to teach English at the secondary school. We will be doing this often, and rotating primary and secondary schools. The kids wear pale yellow collared shirts. The girls wear black skirts, and the boys, pants. Yesterday, our ages were 11-15.

It is an interesting age group, as they have clearly observed the value in knowing English and are very eager to learn it. We went through our French-English picture dictionaries teaching them various basic words, like the parts of the face, colors, animals and such. The kids had a lot of fun and were very engaged. I talked about animals in America, and how dogs are part of the family, often treated like babies, live IN the houses and sometimes even wear clothing. Through that, I taught them English words for dog, baby, house, mom, dad, clothes, etc. They laughed and giggled as I showed them pictures of our dog Pilot, some of her wearing a winter sweater. They giggled and continued to call me "chein man-man" (dog mama). It must seem ridiculous to a culture whose dogs fend for themselves on the street, often dehydrated with protruding rib cages. They are not pets, and are only fed enough to keep them around to bark, should strangers approach. Someone told me that a dog that doesn't bark or shows affection towards people will soon "disappear". The thought is disheartening.

The smiley boy at the orphanage

Bringing chickens home for the family

Bela, one of our kids

Selling dry beans

Jillayna Adamson

Jillayna Adamson

A school

31

1-14-11

Medeline

Medeline is a pretty girl with braided hair and white barrettes. She is the eldest child at our home and is twelve years old, though definitely no twelve by western standards. The other day she took me to watch how she makes dinner. She cooks and cleans every day for the whole family, some cousins, neighbors and anyone else that may be around. The kitchen is a dark outdoor, half open, small stone and clay building with a dirt floor. It quickly grows hot and smoky from the cooking fire. She has a huge bubbling pot of poulet tomat ak pwa (chicken tomato and rice) on a grate over her fire and pours various spices in, eyeing measurements. She sits on a tiny woven chair (cooking chairs, which are seen everywhere) leaning over the pot, and it's not long before beads of sweat form on her forehead and she rests her head against her palm. Haiti is hot. The Haitian kitchen is hotter.

1-15-11

Pre-school and Play

Teaching "ABCs", coloring and a few English words.

Such adorable kids.

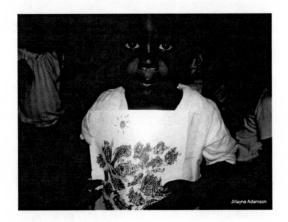

Jillayna Adamson

Sadly, preschools in Pignon are known for their strict punishments and rules, including whips and spankings. For instance, a child would get in trouble for coloring outside the lines of a coloring book, or coloring something the "wrong" color. There is no trace of the "imaginative and creative" guidelines seen in American and Canadian cultures. Obviously, Rod and I did not follow these strict guidelines, and instead encouraged play and exploration. The children were not afraid of us, as they are their teachers.

After a day of teaching, we met up with Donal. Our new friend Donald speaks great English. He is just

17, was born in Pignon, and works supporting his family be doing translations for the UN here. He is always very friendly and helpful to us. We often see him riding alone on the back of the UN truck, and he always invites us to come along. He took us to meet the captain of the UN base here, 'his captain', a friendly Nepalese man. He gave us instant coffee and biscuits and we sat and talked for a while. Before coming to Haiti, he was stationed in Sierra Leone.

The guards all take their stations here with tanks and bulky machine guns. With large helmets and heavy camouflage gear, they seem quite intimidating at first (the guns help). Then you look at the faces behind the helmets and realize how young they are. Young, clean, baby faces that look like they belong in a high school. No doubt, some younger than me.

We were invited back to the base for a Nepalese dinner.

The Quest for Coffee

As an avid coffee drinker, I have been well aware of the days, perhaps even hours, that I have been without coffee. Thus began our quest for coffee....two days ago.

Coffee beans are supposedly a prevalent crop in Haiti, so why on earth couldn't we seem to find coffee anywhere? We asked at little "shops" and "restaurants"-- note, both of these are just huts, people's homes, or makeshift stick tents with a few things stacked inside them.

"Non café," we were told again and again.

Then we met a young, big-boned man who speaks relatively good English, and after speaking with him for a while, he was so enamored with us helping "his country" he said he must in turn help us. So we mentioned that we happened to be looking for coffee...

And so began the journey with Reynold. We wove
in and out of tiny dirt road alleys between little huts
and stands. He stopped to kiss many elderly women
on the cheek, calling them his "second madres".
We heard everybody's stories, about their children,
grandchildren, illness, diabetes in a country with
no insulin, and mothers saving up with high hopes
for their sons to become doctors and help Pignon.
We then learned that our new friend, Reynold, was
studying to become a doctor in Port Au Prince, and
all these old ladies he stopped to introduce us to had
made this possible for him.

After perhaps an hour, we entered a dark hut, and
went into the back, where tiny baby goats galloped
around and naked babies played in the dirt. He led
us into a dark kitchen and introduced us to an old,
hunched woman, telling her we sought coffee. She
brought out a handful of raw coffee beans and ran
them through her fingers before us.

Now, I must admit, I had never seen raw coffee beans before. I didn't even recognize them, and at first protested that we were perhaps misunderstood. Of course, they laughed, and said the old woman would prepare and roast the coffee beans and we could pick them up in two hours.

Two hours later, we made our way back into town, found the old woman's hut, and she handed us a bag of warm, dark, freshly roasted, nutty and bold smelling coffee beans. We paid her and left.

Next step? Grinding the coffee beans. The next day, we asked Medeline—the twelve year old super-child at our house-- to help us. She gathered some of the siblings, who rolled out a large three foot partially hollowed out tree trunk and a large sculpted stick. For about an hour, they pounded at the coffee beans (Rod and I both worked up only a slight sweat as well, trying it out; however they were much more efficient! They all laughed to see a white woman doing it, and it caused some village commotion.) Then they sifted it, poured the coarse parts back in and re-crushed again and again. Two hours later....

Celione brought out what looked like "a dirty sock", according to our new American friend Anthony, which was the filter. She boiled some water and ....Viola! They brought out sugar and cream and we finally had our coffee! Two days, lots of muscle and travel by foot...it was incredibly unique, delicious and well worth it! Such is how it is done in Haiti.

1-18-11

"See over those hills? When the red flag is up, the voodoo doctor is in."

Lave'

On Saturday, we were interrupted in the morning by Celione and the kids who wanted to "lave" (clean) our room. It was quite odd as they all came in, gathered up the sheets and began moving all our things to one side of the room. Unsure exactly what was happening, we just stood and watched. They brought in a broom-- a thin stalk of wood with a giant bushel of straw woven onto the bottom. I offered to help, and while reluctant, they let me. Apparently though, my sweeping was less efficient. They giggled, "non, non, non", grabbed the broom from me, and meticulously swept every inch of our room, shifting our things around. The rest of the family stood at the door, kids and cousins—all leaning on one another and watching.

Then they brought in a (home-made, of course) mop and went to town. Because we were essentially useless, Rod and I just joined the audience at our door. Being that we DO have our own room, I suppose the entire town was curious to see what might be found in a white person's bedroom.

After that, they insisted on washing our clothes. Again, we wanted to at least try to help, and felt uncomfortable simply handing over a heap of our dirty laundry.

The kids all go and fill buckets of dlo (water) from the well and haul them back. They filled giant bowls in the backyard and we sat on the tiny cooking chairs and made our first attempts at Haitian hand-washing

our laundry. Of course, the kids all giggled and point-
ed at us the entire time.

They have a particular scrubbing hand motion they
do that we apparently can't do right (though it
looked the same to me). And let me tell you, they
cover every little inch of EVERYTHING.

Medeline put a cloth in my hand and filled it with tiny
chunks of white Haitian soap. She showed me how
to mold it into a ball with a cheesecloth and rub it
against my wrists. After the clothing is soaked
in the soapy water, you rub it against your wrist with
your knuckles. I must have asked "finis?" fifteen
times, but Medeline was insistent on every article of
clothing that it be absolutely spotless... and every
inch covered. The girl is twelve.

Needless to say, laundry takes ALL day. My wrists
were raw and red, and my hands cramped and tired
by the end. That was only doing MY laundry. Mede-

line does everyone's.

We hung our clothes on cactuses and a clothesline to dry, realizing the day had pretty much gotten away from us, our plans, shot.

On Saturdays, in Haiti, they CLEAN. But... I have never seen my whites so white.

The Second Orphanage and Wizner

Today we visited the Campbell's orphanage, The Haiti Home of Hope. This orphanage, unlike the previous one we've visited, is known to be well run by credible people. Everyone at Haiti Outreach speaks highly of the owners, Bill and his wife, Jennifer.

The orphanage is just outside of town, quite a longer hike from our home, up a curvy dirt hill. We were greeted by a man we had met before, Wizner, who it turns out, works there. This is interesting for a few reasons.

Wizner is handicapped. He speaks very slowly, and with difficulty, and has trouble with motor control of his hands, arms and fingers. They are often cramped up at his mouth, head, or face. I suspect some form of Cerebral Palsy. There are many interesting things about this character. Namely, he speaks incredible English. While we had talked to him before, we did not realize that he worked for the Campbell's orphanage, or even who he was.

People with disabilities in third-world countries are rarely cared for, nurtured, or even given any opportunities. Many of them are abandoned or put in orphanages. Some are feared, as the high belief in witchcraft and voodoo is believed to have been imparted on the mother (thus causing the disability or "curse"). The sad truth is that in most cases, people with disabilities or abnormalities (even simply physical ones) don't stand a chance in cultures like Haiti.

Wizner is 32, and was taken in by American missionaries after being abandoned as a child. There, he learned English, which would later allow him to get a job at the Campbell's orphanage. He told us that the "grace of God" that allowed him to be so fortunate. He is very much aware of that fortune, and is very grateful.

In any event, Wizner showed us around the orphanage. Let me say, the difference is striking. It begins
with the general vibe of the place, the people there.
The kids were playing and giggling, not working.
The babies were being held and rocked. The rooms
weren't completely barren and filthy. Rod and I got
to visit with a baby who was abandoned, most likely
because he has hydrocephalus-- a disease wherein
his head is enlarged because cerebrospinal fluid has
flooded the brain. This disease brings many mental
disabilities. The baby lay in a low crib, and had to
be specially positioned on his stomach with his head
propped to the side. He has a special carriage/wheel-
chair that supports his head for when he is out of
the crib. He couldn't move his head at all, but his big
eyes followed us eagerly, and he occasionally showed
a smile or squeezed my finger.

Rod and I return tomorrow morning and will be there
for the day. Women come in in the morning who

can't breastfeed (or the mother has simply abandoned an infant and they are with another caregiver.
Alarmingly. it is quite common.) and need formula
for their babies. We are helping out in the feeding clinic and spending the day with the kids. I feel
somewhat relieved to have seen this place after seeing the other orphanage....it does give me hope.

1-19-11

L'opital

We brought some supplies to the hospital and were able to talk to some visiting American doctors and a few patients. The doctors told us about the desperation of the hospital, and a lack of supplies. But they didn't need to tell us that, it was obvious before we even stepped inside.

The hospital itself is a few stone and cement buildings guarded by a rusting iron gate. The halls are dark and crowded with sagging beds and IVs lining the walls. Faces poke out at the end of most beds, many of their bodies tiny and frail looking--hardly noticed-- under the sheets. It is loud and chaotic, with various people rushing by, or shouting in fast Creole.

One man had just had his leg amputated. I was able to help a visiting American doctor translate to the

man who lost his leg that she'd visit him that evening but would be going back to the states the next
day. He reached up and hugged her from the bed
and I took a picture for the doctor.

We then met a young woman whose tiny baby was
born that morning. She was beautiful. The doctor told me that the baby was born with no heartbeat and collapsed lungs, but they were able to
resuscitate and stabilize her. Such was lucky, as
she just happened to be born the week the American specialists were there. The mother looked all of
18, but lay in the hallway with the baby next to her
and a big tired smile. She wanted to have the baby's
photo taken. I hope I may find a way to get it to her
someday.

The American doctors explained to us that while
many babies are born each day, it is often a thing
of grief. Rather than a crowd of overjoyed family
members fighting to hold the baby and bringing con-

gratulations, the girls (now new young mothers) are generally alone, in tears and resistant to take their babies home. Some don't. That being said, most women do not go to the hospital to give birth. Death from childbirth—something that is very rarely life threatening in the western world—is much too common in Haiti.

I was grateful that the woman we met was happy, and that the baby's father sat by her side in the hospital. Such is a rarity here.

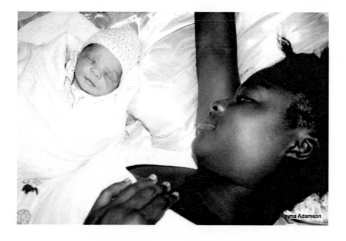

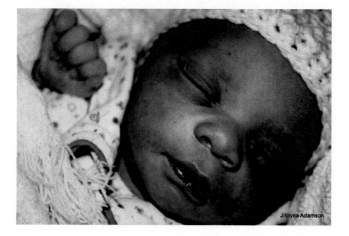

1-20-11

I've mentioned that we live amongst spiders, cock-roaches, mice....

Well, we also live with this:

He is about the size of my hand...

1-20-11

Mikey

Mikey, at one the Campbell's orphanage, is 3 and has hydrocephalus. He is such a sweetheart. He loves to hear his name and listen to us sing songs, to which he clicks along with his tongue. This boy has the smile of an angel.

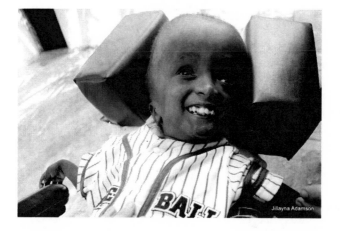

Jillayna Adamson

1-23-11

Edelaine and the Feeding Clinic

The other day, while at the Campbell's Orphanage (AKA, a "good" orphanage), we did work at their feeding clinic. It offers free support for babies and children who aren't getting enough food, protein, are ill or malnourished, or for mothers unable to breast-feed.

Women lined up toting tiny babies, some with slight-ly older babies with chubby cheeks and little rolls of baby fat. Some of the infants were with grandmoth-ers, visibly worn, thin women with sunken cheeks and headscarves. But most of the women in line were quite young.

One at a time, they carried their babies up and hand-ed me folded up, stained index cards with names and dates of previous visits on them. Rod would sift through piles of booklets until finding that baby's re-cords. I lifted them onto little scales, recorded their weights, compared it with their previous visits, and looked them over for any signs of wounds, infection or illness. Then we'd get them two weeks' worth of formula (Free. One weeks' worth if there is suspect-ed illness or noticed weight loss) and we'd write the day for them to return on their index cards. We went through many babies, all warm and cuddly and wide-eyed. Some far too thin. I recorded one visible eye infection-- a poor tiny girl with some swelling and pus around her eyes; one baby with awful sores on his arms and legs, and 5 with weight losses of over 3 pounds in two weeks.

At the end of our session, as all the women were leaving, an older woman showed up with a girl who looked about 6 in height, but was painfully, pain-fully thin. While one of the Haitian men talked to the woman in Creole, I bent down to talk to the little girl. She was bone, her little cheeks and eye sockets sunken in. Her name, she told me, was Edelaine. I picked her up, held her and talked with her as Rod got a new booklet ready for her. I could feel all her rib and hip bones digging into me. Edelaine had never been to the clinic before. As we found out, she'd been abandoned by her mother and left with a grandmother. She was obviously severely malnour-ished. I placed her on the scale and she twirled my hair in her fingers as I held her steady. 23 pounds. One year olds weigh more than that.

I gave her a hug and taught her how to give me a high-five (Haitian kids love this, and we can easily identify kids we've worked with in the area, as they run up and give us a high five or a fist bump.) I had to unclench her tiny fist from a handful of my hair.

We gave her a week's worth of packets of weight gainer foods and supplements and a card for her to return in a week. That poor sweet girl. I've thought about her often since. Would take her home in a heartbeat, if I could.

Rain

Today it began to rain and the busy Haitian streets normally filled with people sitting out and selling goods quickly dispersed. Kids ran wheelbarrows of their family's goods home, and women wrapped up their dry beans and breads in blankets and swarmed into houses. Smaller kids skipped in the street and climbed up on the roofs to watch the dark clouds roll in. Relief, I suppose, after such a hot day. Rod and I were on our way home from town and welcomed it. Though muddier, it's the closest to a shower and some cold air we've had in a while.

1-25-11

Wisly

Wisly bunks in a fair sized, hot and stuffy room with about ten other orphan boys. The beds are bunk beds, relatively bare and saggy, with thin mattresses. He shows us his bed, where he has pictures of various people pinned up to a makeshift bamboo board. Some of the pictures are family members of the Campbell's, and he points and names them for us. He has a small Brazil flag pinned to the ceiling above his bunk, and he says his favorite "football" (American soccer) team is Brazil.

Wisly is fairly light skinned for a Haitian, always smiling and adorably handsome for fifteen. He is somewhat shy, but warms quickly and eagerly asks questions about us, Canada and the U.S. He doesn't hesitate to tell us about his own dreams-- he is the top third student in the 8th grade and he wants to be a doctor-- of this, we are not surprised. He embar-

rasses easily, and looks away after telling us this.

Wisly has been with the Campbell's for eight years now. When he was seven, his mother died and his father had too many kids to care for. And so he "just dropped him off". Watching Wisly though, I don't doubt this turned out for the best. He has gotten to go to school, has learned English from the Campbell's and is quite obviously both a dreamer and achiever. In fact, I was told that he wakes daily at 5:00 a.m. just so he has time to study before chores and school.

Wisly, and 4 other orphan boys led us up Mount Pignon on Saturday. Anthony, Rod and I were sweaty and exhausted; the five boys, however, ran most of the way-- and quite effortlessly. The boys, despite being mostly similar in age to Wisly, obviously look up to him, never questioning any direction or scolding he gave them.

It took two hours to reach the summit, where a cell tower had been put. The boys climbed to the top, again, without so much as a second thought. At the top they sang, hollered and swung their arms. My inner-mother cringed and my heart pounded for fear that one of them would fall or slip. But they'd obviously done this many times. At the top, they tied a cross.

Jillayna Adamson

From a World where People would Die for their Pets... There always seems to be a steady sound of the animal life around us in Haiti. The screeching of roosters or chickens. The baa-ing of goats and the squeals of donkeys and horses hobbling down the roads. Or desperately hungry dogs barking. Tiny puppies whining, attempting to nurse on a starving, emaciated mother.

I have previously mentioned the awful animal treatment here and it's not just the starving, beaten dogs and choked goats. The horses and donkeys carry massive loads nonstop to and from town. While it's quite obvious how poorly they are treated—with whips, open sores and wounds, the loads and the extreme Haitian heat—it was particularly unsettling to learn the details. In fact, as I was told, they rarely feed or give water to the donkeys or horses because they actually become more docile when desperately starving and thirsty. Learned helplessness. The animal treatment here is one of the hardest things to take.

1-25-11

Faces of the Orphans

A runaway child-slave, sold into trafficking around age 6 by his (likely desperate, broke) mother. Managed to run away, and a year ago and was found him curled up outside the orphanage. He is now 11, sweet, and soft spoken. It is terrifying to look into his young eyes and know that there are countless horrible things he's seen and been through.

Girl, victim of the earthquake, where she lost her leg and her entire family. She has been at the orphanage for a year, and is in her teens, one of the oldest girls. A girl, now age 3, was living outside in the sun and dirt of a witchdoctor's home, unfed or cared for as an infant.

Girl, about 9. Her hut caught fire, and her family
died there when she was a toddler. She suffered ma-
jor burns all over her body and face, but managed to
survive. She has been at the orphanage since.

Girl, age 3, getting over cholera and malnutrition.
Mother died, father left her. Been in the orphanage
two years.

Twin girls, age 4, father died, mother was too ill to care for them. She used to visit him, but died while we were there.

Many of the orphans were brought to the orphanage as infants on the brink of death from illness or malnutrition. A few of them have brain damage because of it, and are cognitively impaired in various ways. As someone explained to me, a lot of the kids don't get taken to the orphanage or a hospital until it's "too late".

This boy is cognitively impaired and unable to go to school. He loved to wear Rod's sunglasses and hats and loves soccer.

Jillayna Adamson

Most of the kids in the good orphanages are now
rather healthy physically and mentally. They are all
active, curious, sweet kids. Every one of these kids

has an awful story behind them, either of death, abuse or abandonment. It is hard to look at them, play with them, talk with them and comprehend that they have been through so much. They are just kids. They love to braid my hair and hold our hands. They teach us patty-cake games and love to be silly. They always want to be held or carried, to wear our sunglasses. They love to be spun and tickled. They want to read and go to school and learn. They are kids.

They are the most resilient kids I've encountered.

The kids outside the orphanages are another story. Many of them are at such high risk to die from lack of food and water, be sold as slaves, or abandoned. The desperation of some of these parents for money or food to survive leads them to unbelievable, awful measures.

1-26-11

Edeline

I am incredibly happy to report that Edeline did come to the feeding clinic and has gained two pounds since last week! She was very happy to see me and gave me hugs and big smiles. I gave her some chocolate protein bars, which she was excited about. I was thrilled to watch her gobble them down. I am so glad she was actually fed and brought back...filled with relief. This girl is such a sweetie.

Her cheeks are now more puffed out, and she already looks slightly healthier. Her tiny arm and bloated stomach from being malnourished are somewhat visible in the last image.

The Coffin Makers are always in Business

1-27-11

Clothes

What are the kids in Haiti wearing?

T-shirts, our scraps and the hand-me-downs we
leave in garbage bags outside good-will. Those shirts
you make at Six Flags and Disney World with hearts
and swirlies and your name in bubble letters. A little

boy in a pink shirt that says "Meghan '97". A Cardinals shirt, Pujols. "Number one Dad", a little boy in an oversized, ripped t-shirt. No pants. Often, no underwear. Bums in the dirt and strewn trash. Stained CareBears. "Sexy" in glitter, 8 years old. Phrases, jokes, politics, someone else's' school spirit from 2003. They have no idea. And it doesn't matter.

Ironically, orphans in "good" orphanages are better dressed, as there are actual supporters donating funds or clothes.

1-29-11

Pastor Francois

We decided to bring the bulk of our donations to Pastor Francois' orphanage (another "good" and desperate orphanage).

Pastor Francois is a grandfatherly man with salt and pepper hair, his voice is deep and he speaks in sharp Creole-accented English. (Actually, he kind of reminds me of Morgan Freeman, but that's beside the point.) He is an incredibly kind man with a wife, a white stone church and an orphanage with about 30 kids with very little. They have few outside donors or fundraisers and definitely need all the help they can get. All the kids piled in and gathered around us as we handed out clothes, coloring books, stuffed animals, books, crayons, underwear, bubbles, games, candy cane mice, balls, etc. Many of them only have one or two outfits. They have to wash them every

day - that grueling, hours long, hand-rawing scrubbing. Toys and games are mostly unheard of. There
are only a handful of books. The kids were very pa-
tient and excited. They all watched, holding out their
hands, hugging at their new teddy-bears and pretty
shirts. They held them up to show the others. We
taught them how to blow bubbles. They crowded
around us and sang "God is good" in broken, accent-
ed English. We both tried not to cry.

I have been exhausted, in need of a mental, emotional and physical break. But the truth is, I don't
want to leave.

1-29-11

The Girl Who Can't Walk and a Common Theme

Wizner, from the Campbell's, took us to his bible study group, where he teaches kids songs and bible verses to many tiny kids all the way through teenagers. Under an outdoor stick roof, kids and parents stood waiting, apparently, for us. He brought us over to a little girl in a red dress with braided hair. She sat on a small cooking chair watching us with big eyes. Then Wizner told us that she was six years old, and she couldn't walk. Her mother came over and hoisted her up onto her feet. The girl wobbled and clung to her mother's legs as her mother held her back up. The mother holds another, young baby and she watches me the entire time. Wizner translated for us. Six years old, never walked, no money for a doctor or a wheelchair. Jezebelle. Can't you help?

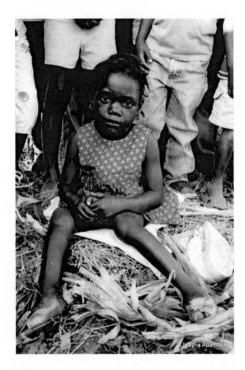

I examined her, best I could not being any kind of doctor. My guess is she could walk one day with physical therapy. Her muscles have atrophied and she has trouble flattening her feet onto the ground. She can stand though, gripping onto someone. She can move her legs. We say we will try to do what we can to get her to see a doctor. But really, as I hold that girl and she wraps her arms around my neck, and everyone watches Rod and I, expecting that we hold the answers and the help they need--I feel entirely helpless. All I know is that if this girl could just come home with me, she'd have a chance, and here, she doesn't. A consistent theme.

Collapse

We smell of bug spray and sunscreen. While constantly eaten by mosquitoes, we never seem to feel them until afterward. They are tiny. We only see the remnants of itchy red lumps up and down our arms and legs. Rod's are getting easily infected, swelling with pus . It is almost impossible to not be dirty here.

It was insanely hot today, making the walks into town and to the schools very tiring. The sky is cloudless and the sun has been relentless. We've slept little in the past few nights. The room is very hot and stuffy. Trying to keep mice and spiders away in complete darkness also adds to that. It's actually easier to sleep in the day because the sun takes so much out of you, especially after walking into town. You essentially just collapse.

However, when the rooster crows at 5 a.m., the day must begin again and the show must go on. There are too many people to help to slow down.

1-29-11

The Feeding Clinic and Chances

We had an amazing day at the feeding clinic. It was packed with mothers, fathers, infants and slightly older kids. At the gate, a group of very old widows sat nursing bandaged arms and holding onto empty stomachs. If there is anything left over after all the kids needing food have gotten theirs, the older people are given some food. They are all thin and hunched, their faces not soft and grandmotherly, but hard, and in tethered, worn wrinkles.

We examined one woman who complained about arm pain, holding her arm cradled against her chest, desperation on her face. You don't even have to know all of what she is saying in crackly Creole to understand the pain and sadness quivering in her voice. She told us her son died recently and she's had little to eat since and few people will help care for her now. She lifted her shirt, showing us her protruding ribs, her dark skin sagging between each bone. Her stomach was concaved, her breasts non-existent. She said she had lost all her weight and now she'd hurt her arm. Tears came to her eyes as she spoke and held onto my hand. Her eyes looked glassy and blue from cataracts.

Her arm was swollen, but likely not broken. We wrapped it anyway. Jennifer told me sometimes, she will do that even if it's nothing truly serious, because sometimes these people just need *something*. Or to feel that someone cares. Even if it is a bit of a placebo, I think it made the woman feel better, and taken care of. That, and her family will likely be sympathetic in seeing bandages and more likely to give

her food. I gave her some soft protein bars and gra-
nola bars. She, like most of the visitors to the weekly
feeding clinic, had walked miles just to get there.

Another woman came up to us holding a tiny baby
in one arm and her breast in the other. I could feel
a huge abscess in her left breast-- it must have
weighed five pounds alone. Jennifer told me that the
woman was certainly in a lot of pain. She had no bra,
and it was so swollen and painful and weighted, that
she had to hold it-- while caring for her new baby.
Unfortunately, she has to keep nursing with her
other breast-- as the milk program for the infants is

entirely full. We gave her antibiotics and painkillers. We got the baby feeding on the other breast, and she bravely tried not to wince. The baby boy was absolutely gorgeous.

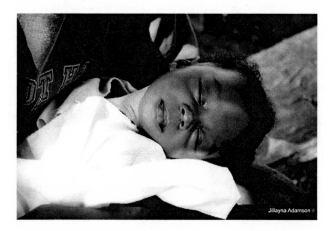

Jillayna Adamson

We saw at least 60 kids and babies. Some days old, still tiny and wrinkled. I loved every minute of holding, rocking, kissing and making them smile. I do believe children are angels; but these children hold a special place in my heart as entirely different forms of angels. I am so thankful they were brought to the clinic and are on the feeding program---so grateful they now have a CHANCE to make it.

But still only a chance
Jennifer told us that from the 2 weeks before we
came, to the first week we worked there, 5 children
who had been on the feeding program died.

Because some of the children are blind or cognitively
impaired from disease or malnutrition, many parents get food from the clinic only to give it to their
healthier kids. A sort of desperate Sophie's Choice,
I suppose. To enforce the rules of taking care of the
kids that need it, the kids are only allowed to stay on
if they are gaining weight and being cared for.
Another type of Sophie's Choice Dilemma for Jennifer to make... Who gets on, who gets to *stay* on.
The kids that need the most help, the parents who
will feed the kids that need it, who aren't lying to
get free food for their *other* kids, or to even sell for
money. These decisions are the type of decisions you
read about in philosophy and morality books.

You can't really get it, until you are there, turning

someone away who is holding a helpless infant because you suspect they are lying, or because there is not enough money to add even a single baby to the program.

A Goodbye Note from Wisly

Wisly is the handsome boy on the right

"Dear Rod and Jill,

Thanks for being a very Good Friend to me! You guys are pretty awesome, and you will be in my prayers always.

Thanks again for the calculator and the other stuff. I'll be missing you guys so much, and I hope to see you again as soon as you can! Have a safe trip my friends. Please say hi to your brother James.

Take care of yourself, my best friends!
PS Hopefully you won't forget my birthday and your
new friend.
GOD BLESS YOU!
Wisly"

Play (Joue')

Running alongside old tires, keeping them in-line with sticks. Alarmingly universal hand-clapping games. Home-made kites that kids fashion out of trash. Wheel-barrow rides.

Love

Our time is drawing to an end. We are dirty, and exhausted physically, mentally and emotionally. It has been an amazing trip, and it will be very hard to leave. We've met so many incredible people.

Me, with some of our family. I love these kids.

Bottom row L-R: Gamonelle and Cee (Wenciez)

Top row L-R: Bela, Sabine, moi, Medeline, Kiki

The Hardest Part is coming Back

When Rod and I went to Haiti, there was never any culture shock. We didn't go into depressions or cry ourselves to sleep. We didn't look back, feel scared, or in any way doubtful of our decision to go. We just fit in, easing into the lifestyle, the people. We made quick friends and met families and children that we were instantly in love with. We formed a months worth of bonds and attachments. We got used to the tarantulas, to being constantly dirty (ok, that was a bit of an adjustment), to hard working days on our feet under that brutal sun.

The culture shock was coming back. It was seeing Reese Witherspoon on People Magazine--something about her love life. It was stores, endless rows of "stuff", of food--just sitting there. Streams of SUVs. Grocery stores, crammed with people casually push-ing overflowing shopping carts while on their blu-etooths. Little kids throwing tantrums over the M&Ms

their mum won't buy them in the check-out line.
(And then, she rolls her eyes and throws it on the
counter anyway.) Microwave pizzas. Hot showers. I
could go on forever.

We have found ourselves in a bit of a funk, shell
shocked, and overwhelmed by this strange world.
I feel, almost homesick. Guilty. The entirety of my
thoughts since my return have revolved around my
kids in Haiti---around how and when I will get back.

So Now What?

Of course, we are going back. My heart is now in Haiti in the hands of all those kids. It was so impossibly hard to leave, to hug and kiss all those kids goodbye. To get on that tiny plane and watch all those people waving at us get smaller and smaller. The only question is when. We are hoping for another trip this year.

Thanks to all of you guys, here is where the remainder of our raised funds are going:

An education fund for our families kids to ensure they ALL get to finish school. Currently, only roughly half of them are in school, and there is not enough money to even finish school.

We are also starting an education fund for the little girl. I've fallen in love with Edline. She is not in school, and that will change. We will also ensure that she stays on the feeding program.

In the meantime, with our own money, I am putting together a birthday present to send down for Wisley's upcoming 16th birthday, and a care package with clothes, toys and dolls for Eldine

Me and my brother, James

Survival

I love the simplicity of life in Haiti. It is remarkable the way people work to survive. The kids are smart and skilled and responsible. They start learning how to carry objects on their head around age 4, after all. But there is also a strange air of relaxation constantly around. She a contrast from the fast paced life of America and Canada.

In Haiti, everyone is just trying to SURVIVE. They are literally just trying to get enough food and water for themselves and their family. Every day revolves around that. Every. Day.

In the west, in most cases, we are well past survival. We are on to "thriving", bettering ourselves emotionally, mentally and intellectually. Survival is a given— we are seeking more. Constantly, more. We are self-focused, we believe in "alone-time", "me" time, reflection and building the self. But here, they are busy. A busy you have never known: survival busy. They eat big spaghetti meals for breakfast because they work hard in fields and on the streets in the hot sun all day. They are just hoping they can get enough money to get through a day. It is one day at a time. There is no future, no plans—because you must first get through today. And there is sure as hell no "quit", no vacation time, no sick or personal days.

They don't eat diner. They save food for when it's physically needed for working—breakfast and lunch. There is no obesity; there is no "food addiction" or eating when you're bored.

It is hard for me to explain from a standpoint of always having had more than enough, just how what these people DO have is perceived. Food is god. Water is god. An eight year old girl can walk 3 miles up a steep hill balancing a 10 pound water bucket on her head because she HAS to to survive. There is no "want" here. Everything people have, they have worked tirelessly without complaint for. Such is all they know. Their whole life. Survival.

Final Thoughts

"Give a man a fish and you feed him for a day. Teach a man to fish and you feed him for a lifetime." **Chinese Proverb**

There are generations in Haiti that have unfortunately grown up on "hand-outs" from missionaries and visitors. They've learned that white people seem to have money and capabilities far beyond their means. So, they beg. They do "favors" for you, always with high expectations of something in return. Not everyone is like this, of course. But there are even people well-off to Haitian standards who will still bother and follow every white person they see. Eventually, some of them become unhealthily reliant and unable to help themselves.

One hospital employee followed us home one day, entirely sure that we had "something" for him. And this man had a job, had training-- that's so much more than many people have there.

We learned that it is important not to just give things or money away to kids you see in the streets. This is why we gave to orphanages and the family we were staying with. Imagine the feeling of a parent when their little kid able to come running home with something so easily, when they work hard, non-stop-- just trying to feed them. Many of them need to learn skills---not just get handouts. Many projects, buildings and wells go to waste because the Haitian people don't know how to manage and maintain these things. They get destroyed and broken down. They are not taught what the western world views as traditional management and responsibility in a busi-ness sense. Haiti Outreach works to teach and imple-ment skills in maintenance and management so that these people can keep things going that they do get. So that they work for it, respect it, and value it as something that is a part of their community.

In the past, people have tried to bring electricity to Pignon, a plan that always fails because the Haitians don't have the skills or money to continue to maintain and run it. It's great to donate such things, but one must help Haiti to help themselves.

Currently, Haiti Outreach is attempting to put a clean water system throughout the entirety of Pignon. There is also a road project in the process, so that it is easier to travel within and to/from Pignon. We heard of tons of pounds of food that sat to rot in Port Au Prince after the earthquake as there was no way to get the food to Pignon. Food that absolutely could have been used.

We will continue to help, continue to give and aid where we can to those that are truly in need. But it is more than giving that must be done. It is loving, teaching, investing. To send a check is not enough, it is not the end. We have all heard the saying. In Haiti, it's not just doing your math homework for your kid, who will never learn math himself. It is survival.

The Return in 2012

July 2012

We are safe and sound in Pignon and so unbelievably happy and excited to be back.

When we stepped off our little plane, there were so many familiar faces there waiting to greet us. So many hugs and so much excitement. It was wonderful.

My little Bela (Bay-la) came running to me and jumped into my arms. Man, how this sweetheart has grown!

Always a Setback

It Haiti, there always seems to be significant setback with anything you try to do. For starters, the airline lost the one bag we checked....a bag with tons of our donations and food (amongst other things). Luckily, we both have our huge hiking backpacks with us and we were able to carry those on.

It is not exactly easy to get a missing bag (even if found) to a remote town in the middle of Haiti from Port Au Prince. One that you have to take a 4-person charter plane to get to. They seemed to think they could get it to us today or tomorrow, so we are remaining hopeful.

Not surprisingly, we have been busy and I have seldom been around internet connections. It's wonderful to be back here, back among friends and back into the Haitian life. Flying in to Pignon from Port we could already feel it—the simplicity, the calmness, the beauty in everything. The mountains were even greener and more beautiful than we remembered.

A few things have changed in Pignon over the last year. The good with the less good. There are some partially paved roads in town. A few more places with scattered electricity. New faces at Haiti Outreach, and Bill and Jen's orphanage as well.

You might remember Medline from my previous stories last year. We lived with a local family and Medline was the oldest daughter (12). She was amazing and took care of everyone. Essentially a little mother and caretaker...she cooked, cleaned, took care of the younger kids...She was about a million times more responsible and mature than I am....And definitely not your western twelve year old. I had heard, prior to our trip, that Medline (the oldest daughter in the family we stayed with in 2011) was no longer living with her family. I was not given an explanation about this. Because of that, I was worried. Had she been married off? Medline is such a sweet, intelligent and motivated girl...but if her family got an offer from someone promising to take care of her or the family...well, they don't always have room for decision making.

And so...Medline is gone. We haven't really gotten too far on an explanation...but apparently she went with her birth mother (Celione is her mother, but not birth mother. It is not uncommon for Haitian kids to live with other 'mothers'). I am hoping this is a good thing, but I really am not sure. I do know she is no longer in Pignon. If her birth mother is able to care for her, I sure hope she is still in school and pursuing the things she told us she wanted to.

It is odd not having Medline at the house. It is now Celione (the mother—who is still as tiny as ever), Sabine, who is 9, Bela who is 4, Gamonelle, who is 3. Then Dzioli, who must be about 17, Kiki who is 7 and two new babies that are not Celione's but are somehow related. There is also a young girl, likely 19 or 20, and I suspect she is the mother of one or both infants. I think much of the care-taking is now on Sabine. She is still sweet, still playful, but I already note a different air of seriousness and maturity.

Sabine, 9

Celione's husband worked for Haiti Outreach. He died shortly after the earthquake when his car went off a cliff. The people in town call her Madamme Leonard, referring to her now 'widow' status (they also call her 'the widow'). But she can't be much older than Rod and I, if at all. After his death, Haiti Outreach gave Celione a job as a cook in the guesthouse to be sure she'd be able to take care of all her children.

While we are not staying there this time, we are visiting often. The kids have grown, but are all still very much the same. They all stood in the field watching as our plane landed and ran to us. It was like being swarmed by a tiny village.

So many friends came out to see us arrive. I suspect that word that we were coming got around, as it tends to do in Haiti.

After our hugs with Donal, he quickly...quite delightfully...that I had gotten 'fatter'. This was his way of complementing me. In Haiti, it is not, 'Nice to see you, you look great', its 'nice to see you, you've gotten fatter!'. He motioned toward my hips, almost excited. (For my own psychological wellness...I am still wearing the same size jeans ...so unless I am delusional, I am going to say he was just being 'polite'...) Donal showed us the tiny 'farm' (it is more of a garden) he is working on growing crops with the help of an American who purchased some land for his family to work. He was excited and wanted pictures. It is a huge deal that he was able to get barbed wiring around it and he is quite proud. (Donal is about 17 and speaks awesome English...he was a great friend to us last year).

Even on our first day back, we have met people eager to tell us of their ailments, eager to know if we can help them. We've been stopped in the street, not just over the excitement at the fact that we are white (and seeing a white person is such a rarity here...and some children have never seen one. I almost forgot that I already immediately react to the name 'blanc'!), but because we are white...and those assumptions are in place that we must be able to help. An old woman limped after me, telling me of the pains in her leg. I stopped and talked with her, sympathized, held her hands...but it was really all I could do. She thanked me as if I'd worked miracles, while I apologized for my helplessness. Really, she thanked me for listening. Caring. Stopping for a few minutes. These types of encounters are common-place.

The reality is, we are not much. I am back in that space where I wade between feeling absolutely help-less and useless to feeling that I am able to con-tribute, help or make some kind of a difference. Its a thin line here. You see so much, and you have to know and understand that you cannot 'fix' it all. And sometimes you can't do anything.

An Update on the Campbell's

It's been great to revisit Bill and Jennifer and all the kids at their orphanage. While there are a few new additions, there were quite a few faces happy to see us. I handed out photographs I had taken of some of the kids—they were very excited about this (many of them haven't seen or have never had pictures of themselves). We held babies, played with the older kids, toured the new girls' house and dining hall. They have come quite a ways in a year. The kids are still so happy and playful, they want to hang off us, get their pictures taken, wear our hats and sunglasses. Many of them have notably spurted over the course of a year.

One of the children that we had spent a fair amount of time with last year was Desoli. Desoli had some learning disabilities. I am not entirely sure in what ways he was cognitively impaired, but he definitely functioned on a lower, more elementary level. Desoli was very playful and social. He spent a lot of time around Rod and I last year (there are pictures of him playing with Rod's hair and dressing up in his clothes).Desoli turned 17 this year, and while it's something of a long story, he attempted to try a life outside the orphanage. It is with great sadness that I write that our friend Desoli passed away this year. He became ill with cholera quickly after leaving the orphanage. Rod and I were shocked to hear this, and incredibly saddened.

Desoli and Rod in 2011

Mikey (the adorable, happy boy at the Campbell's who has hydrocephalus) is also not doing well. With his condition (especially in Haiti), he is not expected to live a very long life. He is about 4 now, and has been quite sick. He is now living in Bill and Jennifer's home with them, getting extra care. That said, Jennifer reported that while they thought he was dying the past few weeks, he has shown some progress over the last few days.

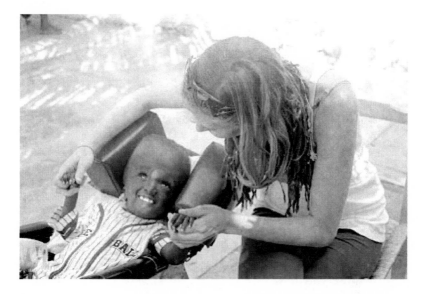

Mikey

Lavi is a the new baby at the orphanage. She is an adorable tiny little thing with big eyes and a head full of curls. Lavi is three months old, but about the size of a newborn. She came to the Campbell's premature at 2 lbs after her pregnant mother (with some serious mental illness) attempted to cut her out of her stomach with a razor blade. Lavi is doing well though, and has been gaining weight.

It is no surprise to Rod and I how well Wisly continues to do. He's as handsome as ever, and is still incredibly enthusiastic and affectionate. It was wonderful to spend time with Wisly, who is going to be 16, is in the 9th grade, and excitedly told us that he got the highest grade in his government exams. We are not surprised. Wisly was up early daily studying, and we hardly saw him for a few days. We'd catch him riding his bike down the dirt road back to the orphanage after a day of studying, or hours of intense test taking. Always smiling. He never once complained about the testing, about studying, about school. And yes, Wisly still proclaims that he will be a doctor. I have no doubts in him. If ever someone who came from little to nothing could achieve their dreams, it's Wisly.

This little honey on my lap came in incredibly
malnourished and impaired from that.
She is 5 or 6 years old.

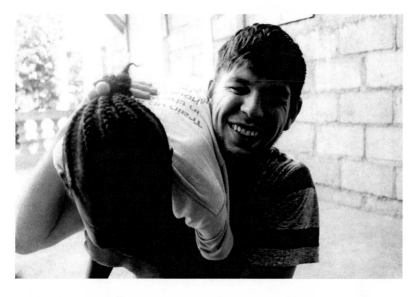

Tomorrow is the feeding clinic. I am both excited and discouraged (as we have lost so much of our stuff...I am hoping we might hear about it tomorrow, or perhaps, that by some miracle, it will be here.)

Ah well, we will do what we can with what we have. We found a woman who is going to make us a big tub of mamba (peanut butter) and a few loaves of bread to feed the people who have walked all that way to the clinic. We will also pass out what clothing, toys and bars we do have. Not to mention, we will get some kids set up for the feeding clinic thanks to our awesome donors!!

The Feeding Clinic

In good news, we got our bag (yesterday) morning...
just before the feeding clinic! Thank god. Perfect tim-
ing.

The clinic went very well this morning and we saw a
number of kids, infants and elderly widows. All the
kids got lots of vitamins, clothing, stuffed animals,
coloring books, meals and food to snack on.
People lined up outside the little clinic, holding and
comforting crying or awe-struck infants and children,
waiting for their turn. Once called in, I weighed the
babies and kids and Jennifer recorded their new
weights in their booklets. Always hoping and praying
for a gain. I then took the kids, gave them snacks,
some gummy vitamins, picked out a stuffed animal or toy as well as some clothing. The kids were
happy to get their stuffed animals and most of them
couldn't take their eyes off them. They loved the

kid's vitamins (I'm sure they taste like candy) and one little boy kissed me on the cheek and asked for more. Many of the children are not taken care of by their parents, nor were they brought to the clinic by their parents. Some of them came in with grandparents, or random people in their village. Some with brothers and sisters who couldn't be more than 10. The majority of the people at the clinic had walked in many miles from neighboring villages, toting naked, sweaty babies on their hips.

I met with one little girl, likely 3, who has AIDS and two parents also with AIDS. While she has been gaining weight, she has a number of sores all across her body. Her name is also Edeline. She was sweet and quiet and had been brought by an uncle. She was enamored with the stuffed bear we gave her, and the dresses. I fed her some protein bars and fruit snacks and she quietly said 'merci' a number of times.

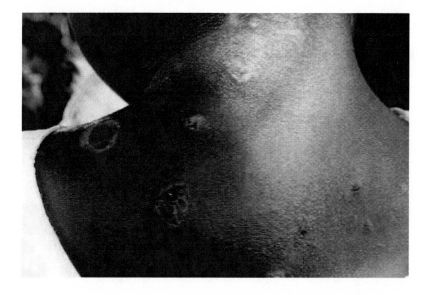

There were many young kids suffering impairments, likely the result of malnourishment. Many were still bony and knobby, but steadily gaining a very small amount of weight. For those that hadn't gained any weight since the last clinic, or who had lost weight, we had to look into whether the food given has not been given to the child, is being withheld, or if the child has another existing illness.

I half fell in love with a pretty little girl who had walked many miles to bring her two brothers (one,

an infant, the other only slightly younger than her).
I later learned that the infant has AIDS and the family refuses to believe it, even when offered treatment which is incredibly effective if started so young. The girl was ten and had these gorgeous light brown eyes. She wore a long tattered dress and had her infant brother on her hip. Her other brother, perhaps 7 or 8, had the same light colored eyes, but had pink sores around them. Fruit flies buzzed constantly around them. Jennifer told me that the parents of these children are incredibly neglectful. Right now, the girl is at a high risk of being trafficked. Jennifer said she wouldn't be surprised if her mom sold her.

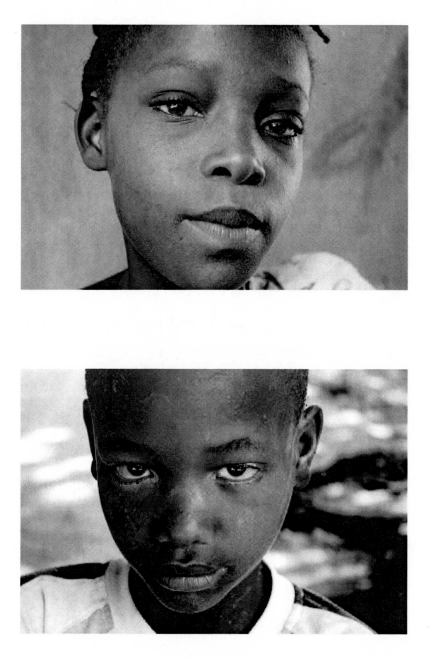

She had small braids that were being started at the back of her head—something done that tends to make kids look more sexualized and attractive. Likely, her parents were having these braids put in. The last thing that girl needs is to look older or prettier. She is at such a high risk right now, that we had to be careful when picking out clothing for her--- anything too short or too low or had to be avoided. No shorts, and only long dresses. The girl does all the caretaking for her siblings, and it seems that her parents often withhold food, and possibly allow family or village members to do awful things to her. I gave her some clothing and a stuffed animal, some food and a backpack. We gave the boy some toys and protein bars for their walk back home. She was a sweetheart, and I really wished I could just whisk her away from all of it. It was hard to watch her walk back out the gate knowing that all these possibilities were upon her.

Bugs, and other things on the Back Burner

We wake up with bugs in our bed. Sometimes, little flying things that are dead and we have squished in our sleep. Sometimes, just content little lord-knows what's lounging on our pillows. We do so much walking everyday along the rocky, dirt (blister giving) roads in the baking sun, and often by the time we return to the home we are staying at, it hardly matters that we are blistered, lined with dirt and sweat and can smell ourselves. Nor do we seem to notice that the jugs of clean water we bring with us must be at least body temperature. (Add hauling a twenty pound hiking backpack on top of that. You'd have never drank so much water in your life. There is only one place we can get clean water, so we try to savor and ration. But sometimes thirst takes over and you can hardly stop yourself from downing an entire jug.) Much in the same ways that it comes to matter little when we lay down amongst the bugs.

At night, if we happen to wake up, (which we don't often, as we are nearly unconscious from the day's efforts), the ceiling in our room is lined with small swirling, glowing bugs. They are bright and green... much brighter than any lightning bugs I've ever seen. When we first saw them, I wondered if maybe we were dehydrated and seeing things. Or overly tired. They swirl around in fast circles and it's quite odd, but neat to watch.

We are quite lucky, because we are staying in a home that has electricity (lights) and a toilet this time. Still bathing in a little basin we fill with water, but we have running water! So, we are being slightly spoiled this time around. That said, we are only at the house at night, to sleep...so are not around to enjoy these luxuries so much!

We took a motorbike into town with our supplies for the clinic, myself sandwiched between a sweaty

Haitian guy, hugging my arms around him for dear life, and Rod behind me gripping onto me with two full backpacks on him. He weaved around rocks and donkeys and hit slightly jolting bumps, honking at anything in his way before slowing. When trying to get off the bike, I fell against the exhaust pipe and I have myself a nice burn. It is already oozing pus, peeling, and raw, so Rod and I have been trying to keep this thing as clean as possible. It's far too easy to get an infection down here. Thus far, only a couple minor battle wounds for us. Such is promising.

A Few kids at the Clinic/ Feeding Program

Mother has died of AIDS. She is negative, steadily gaining weight on program.

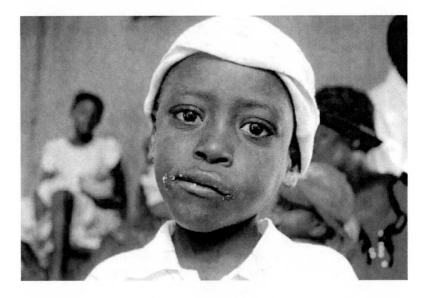

Still very underweight, but no longer malnourished.

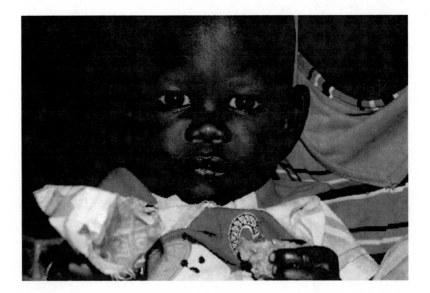

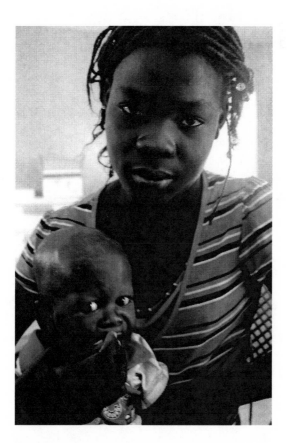

Lost weight, currently extremely neglected by

mother. Mostly cared for by this sister.

Finding Edeline

Today, we journeyed for half a day to find Edeline. Edeline recently came off the feeding clinic and is doing well, but we continue to keep her in school. I haven't seen her since she came to the clinic, age 5, weighing 23 lbs.

We knew that finding Edeline was going to be a challenge. She lives with her grandmother in a neighboring village quite a ways away. And it's not as if there are addresses to go to or phone numbers to call. We had the name of a village, and a year old picture of a very malnourished little girl. And a name.

And so, off we went, with Pastor Clabar, white knuckled as we all piled onto his four wheeler. We rode for perhaps 20 to 30 minutes. 20 to 30 minutes of bumps and jolts, minor whiplash and serious bumbruising happening. He swerved around goats and muddy ditches, slowing slightly for the extreme bumps.

When we finally arrived in the area, all we could do was go from person to person, holding her cute little picture and asking if they knew where we might find her. Clabar stopped the 4 wheeler, talking to locals in Creole—of which Rod and I were able to pick up some of, but they spoke fast and often on top of one another. More and more people began to gather, circling around us. Her picture passed from hand to hand, adults and children alike. Most people shook their heads or stopped and seemed to be deep in thought. They all watched us with big eyes, and the kids came running out to us shouting to the others that there were 'blancs' in the street. The crowd grew. Edeline's picture went around and conversation between the village people was heated. Eventually, we got nowhere, and headed further down the road.

I started to become discouraged. I had been so sure

we'd be able to find her. Surely, someone had to know where she lived or recognize her. I found myself searching the faces of every child in the street, or children walking by. I became afraid I wouldn't recognize her. Afraid she has grown and is unrecognizable to what she looked in her malnourished state. When the second group of Haitians didn't recognize her, my mind began to wander to terrible places. What if she had been sold into slavery or killed? What if something awful has happened to her?

We found her school, and I walked around the grounds. It's a fairly small tin building with a little white church next to it. School is out for the summer, but it gave me hope to know that she had been in this same space. We finally came across some people who were working to build a house. One of them knew the principle of the school. He said he would try to find a telephone, because the principle had a cell phone. My hopes started to raise again, but I still felt so nervous that we'd leave the village without having found this precious girl.

Another group led us to a home, claiming they knew where to find Edeline. My hopes were high. The little girl that came out was not my Edeline, but her name was Edeline. She was around the same age and had the same build. Again, my heart dropped.

Fast forward twenty minutes. We sat outside her school in the sun. The principle was supposed to come meet us there. We waited and waited. It is vital to know that Haitian minutes are useless. People will tell you they will be there in 'two minutes'. Well two Haitian minutes is equivalent to about an hour. Needless to say, a tall man came riding in on a motorbike. We ran to him with Edeline's picture. He smiled and nodded. I could have cried then.

We followed him on his motorcycle to a tiny path at the base of the mountain. We would have to walk from here. We hopped off, and began walking along a dirt path, the mountain straight above us, corn fields all around us. There wasn't a house in sight. After walking for a while, we began to see little huts between stalks of corn. The principle led us to a little stick gate, which we were instructed to climb. We were on a thin path in a cornfield, which we were to follow to her home. Little kids at the home saw us, and began to run out. They all looked up at us, and I searched their faces for Edeline. Nothing.

Finally, we approached a little clay house in the middle of the tall corn field. We couldn't have seen that from the dirt road. An older woman came over to us. Her hair was grey and matted. She had on a skirt and no shirt. Her breasts sagged down before us. She held up a finger, motioning toward her chest. She disappeared inside the house, returning with a shirt on, chuckling at us, but noticeably confused at the white people outside her home. Pastor did the bulk of the translating for us. I looked around, still anxious.

Then, a little head poked out from inside the house. A beautiful, familiar little face. For a second, I could hardly breathe. Edeline was taller, her face more filled out. She looked healthy! She smiled! She looked up at me with that same look. It was priceless.

I was quickly on my knees. I gave her the picture I had taken of her last year at the clinic. She smiled, giggling. We had a number of things for Edeline, including a backpack, stuffed animal, coloring books, French-English children's dictionary, crayons, pencils, toys, jump ropes, a little candy and lots of dresses and clothes. She was adorable and excited and scooped up each item, trying to hold it all. I held her and kissed her little cheeks, asking about school, about how she was. She showed me her grade card from school. Rod and I also bought a giant tub of Haitian Peanut Butter (mamba), which we had specially made in Pignon for Edeline and her family. Peanut butter is expensive, but an excellent source of fats and protein. I knew it was unlikely that her grandmother was able to afford it for her and her little cousins. I showed her and she gasped and said "Yum!".

We spent a little time there, took some photos. I told her how happy I was to see her healthy, and to eat lots of mamba. She hugged me again, still holding onto one of her stuffed animals.
We will continue to put her in school.

It is amazing, but we found Edeline. She is happy and giggly and healthy. She is beautiful, and has grown so much in a year. My heart hurts. I am so thankful that the stars aligned for us to see her again.

Take a look:

My precious Edeline came to me a year and a half ago weighing 23 lbs and very malnourished.

Her eyes were sunken in, her rib cage protruding, and her little stomach puffed out in starvation.

Now Edeline is happy and healthy and has finished up her 2nd year of school, doing incredibly well.

She is just beautiful.

A Few Photos

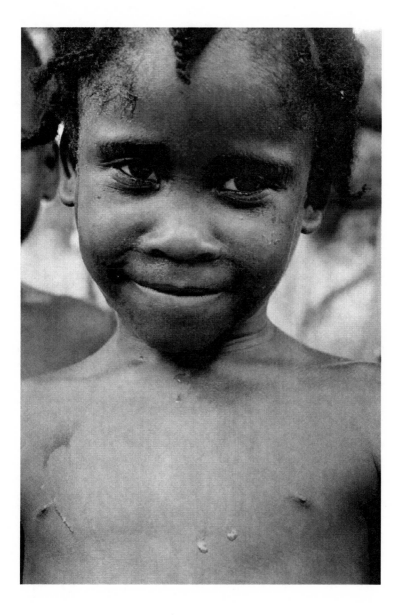

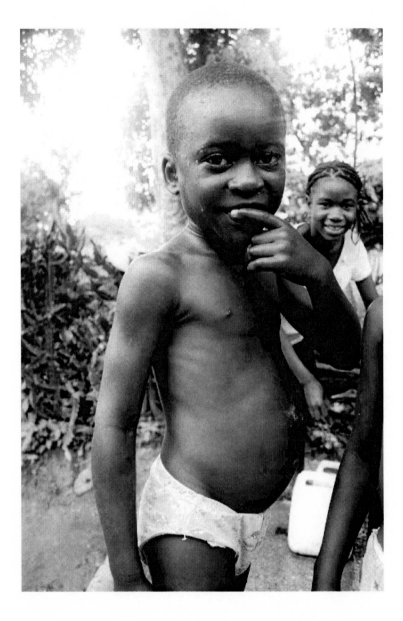

Mamba! Haitian homemade peanut butter (just put in some random container)! We love this stuff...ate quite a bit of it last year! Very different from American Peanut Butter. It should be noted, though (as per my education through Meds and Food for Kids), that you must be careful about the Haitian peanut butter, as not all peanut growers are using the most sanitary or high-health standard methods—simply out of a lack of education about healthy, safe farming methods.

We are headed to Pastor Francois' orphanage (you may remember from last year, he is the grandfather-ly man who reminds me of Morgan Freeman. Last year, we gave the bulk of our donations to the kids there and they sang us an adorable, heartbreaking song.) We are going back to visit and have a number of donations for them as well.

Today we ask around to find a ride for Cap Haitien tomorrow, a city a couple hours away. Likely, we will be on the back of a motorbike, or if lucky, in a car or truck. It will be a bumpy ride, as there are no paved roads.

We plan to head there in the morning. Once there, we will meet with Patricia Wolff of Meds and Food for Kids and tour the new Medika Mamba factory and learn more about what she is doing in Cap Haitien.

That makes this our last day in Pignon. It is bitter-sweet, and we have many people to go visit with. Not quite ready to say goodbye yet.

The Widows

The Widows wait outside the feeding clinic, hoping to get even the slightest bit of food or comfort that might be left over for the kids. I have written about them before. I visited with many of the same widows as last year. Still hungry and sore with countless aches and pains. Still playful and friendly. But quietly desperate. C'est Haiti.

Jillayna Adamson

Jennifer received a number of donations so that each of the widows also took home a quilt. Unfortunately, they are not highly valued by family members (if they have them) and seen as a drain on resources. They don't get the food, medical attention or comfort that they need. They love to have their photos taken, to tell you of their aches and pains.

We handed out baggies of vitamins...while they certainty can't hurt, and may help a bit with each of their states of health, their primary effect, I imagine, is a placebo. We give them bags of pills, they hold their hands out, eager to get their bag of medika (medicine). We strictly tell them one per day, and to swallow with food. We tell them it's for their aches and pains, their sores-- whatever it is they need to hear. We point to their achy legs or bruised ribs, the bones that never healed quite right in their foot, their cataracts. Such is what they need. While the amount the vitamins can actually help may be small in comparison to what they are expecting, it does seem that they are able to thrive and keep going with the knowledge of others' care and concern. With whatever it is these 'blancs' have, that must surely be magic. I suppose, in that sense, it is.

Afterwards, they laugh and ask to have their photos taken. They love this, and giggle as they see their own face on my camera. They point out their wrinkles and the sags in their skin and they insist all their friends see as well. They laugh when I say the pictures are beautiful. I imagine they think I am humoring them. But really, these old women, they are the rocks of the children The caretakers of children left behind. Beyond the state of walking 5 miles to get to the feeding clinic, and yet they do.

That is not your average woman. It is a strong, beautiful survivor. One that keeps playing the care taking role, even when no one is caring for them.

Jillayna Adamson

Hitchin' a Ride

We asked around in Pignon, looking for a ride to Cap Haitien, about 2 hours north of Pignon. A ride to Cap Haitien (where we have more business to take care of, and fly out of), most suredly means being packed elbow to elbow standing in the back of a truck, or hugging onto some guy on the back of his motor-bike. We ended up choosing the later, preferring to be taken directly where we were staying, rather than just dumped into the city and having to find our way around.

Finding someone willing to take us on this 2 hour journey was the easy part.

And so, Rod and I piled on behind a Haitian man with our two moderately heavy hiking backpacks full of all our stuff. The roads (as we knew, and as is common in Haiti) we unpaved, rocky dirt roads. The much needed rainstorm the night before left many shin-deep dark-brown puddles, that our escort rode through, as our feet and ankles went underwater. A few times, we were motioned off to push, and Rod had to wade through what became a river—though he insisted on finding a moderately shallow part to ride through with me. I was ankle deep, and we moved slowly, but our driver was pleased with his chivalry.

To get from Pignon to Cap, we had to go over two mountains. In case you forgot, we were on a little motorbike, our bums definitely bruised, our backs and necks constantly jolted from the ceaseless bumps. Sticking a couple mountains in there only made it that much more of an adventure. Laying on your horn, while going around the bend of a make-shift dirt path winding down the mountain—in case you are wondering—is the number one safety mea-sure. We managed not to hit goats, donkeys and people traveling with large baskets of goods or jugs of water on their heads. But it wasn't uncommon to feel them graze your arm as you passed, or to pull your knees in when going by a truck. There is no point of relaxation, but rather a constant bracing for the next jolt, or preparing to lean at the next turn.

(Don't mind the state of the pictures. There's no slowing down on Haitian roads.)

First mountain to climb

My poor husband carried the bulk of the weight on his back for the two and a half hours the ride took us. We passed through many country sides, little villages of people whose children called out to us and others who stopped to stare. The bike was old and noisy, and he stopped once instructing us to get off to hit the wheel repeatedly with a broken pop bottle—I'm sure he had his reasons.

Finally, we made it into the hectic city, and had to thread in and out of alleys and streets and up and down another mountain to our hotel. Our driver had asked for 800 gouds (Haitian money) for this trip. Bemused at our amazement of making it in one piece on that rusty old bike, we have him 1000 gouds. His smile at this was huge, and he showed that he was grateful. When we got into our room, we couldn't help but notice in the mirror (first of all, there was a mirror!) that save for the outline of our sunglasses, our faces had been evenly sprayed with a coat of chalky brown dirt. (We are going with dirt). 1000 gouds, you should know, is $25 American dollars.

In Cap Haitien, and the Medika Mamba Mission

I can't say that we knew where we were staying when we went to Cap Haitien. We had looked up a few places---really had an option of three or four, and picked the one we could actually get a hold of and get information about. Turns out, it's probably the nicest (or only nice place) in Cap. It is past the city over another mountain that houses small bundles of homes and shacks. Once you're over the mountain, and you make it to the base, you are at a beautiful ocean. Perhaps the gods had it in store for us to get some relaxation in on the next part of our venture. The place was practically a resort on the beach with clear, warm ocean water. There were lights, running water, toilets—and a shower! A few people even spoke English.

We managed to get a car to take us to meet with Pat (Dr. Patricia Wolff of Medika Mamba/ Meds and Foods for Kids). They were in the process of finishing up their new, much bigger factory for producing the malnourishment product.

We talked at length about Pignon, about Haiti, about children and malnourishment and other relating fundamental problems. She took us to tour the factory that was now closed, so that Rod could look over all of the engineering in the equipment. Their set up was small, basically the size of a middle class American home. The peanut butter medicine was made and packaged there, the lab tests done, and all the other little things that come into making, packaging and distributing a product. All squeezed into that building, employing about 30 there alone.

She showed us an outside patio area where they dried the peanuts, storage areas and the other tedious nooks and crannies needed for the product to be made safely and effectively.

The expanded factory is 10 times in size, and as you can imagine, will employ a much larger number of factory workers, lab workers, farmers, etc. It could do great things for the Haitian economy. All these people must be carefully trained and educated - as the equipment is largely foreign and advanced to them, as well as many of the principles of work ethic and responsibility, rules and regulations that exist in such a field. It is no small feat.

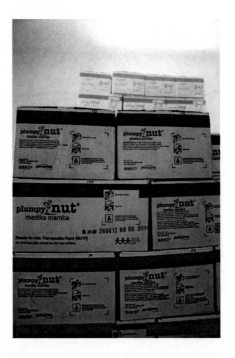

The good news is we have basically gotten it set up to get Medika Mamba to Pignon. It's not there yet, and we are still working out some bugs, but it is going to happen and the wheels are now in motion!

This will make children recover and get over the hump of malnutrition much faster than traditional methods—which take 6-8 MONTHS to get a child to a relatively healthy weight.

With Medika Mamba, it will take 6-8 WEEKS, and will bring in more vitamins, minerals, fats and protein!

I have been incredibly excited to learn about the organization Meds and Food for Kids and the amazing things that Dr. Wolff is accomplishing to help Haitian children (in addition to the economy). The peanut butter product is an amazing and feasible solution to get these kids over that incredibly difficult extreme malnourishment phase without hospitalization. We will leave Cap Haitien in hopes that our work with MFK is just beginning. And we leave knowing that our work in Haiti is in its beginning stages, and remains full of hope and possibility.

Haiti isn't that Far Away, but it's a Long Way Down

A Final Note

We returned from Haiti with the same unsettling sense of 'culture shock' that we previously experienced upon returning to the states. However, it was slightly lesser, and was expected. We were prepared for it, but had little time to adjust before being thrown back into the western world, our full time jobs and regular day to day duties.

Haiti might be a third world country. It might be a nation that struggles endlessly with poverty and corruption, but Haiti is a place of beautiful, extraordinary people. Haiti struggles to navigate in a modern world of high technology and changes. It is a nation with a rich history that I urge anyone and everyone to become educated on to help understand why Haiti is what it is today. And why Haitians are the people they are.

Rod and I go down to Haiti with our western education, we know facts and figures, we have skills and knowledge that has been engrained in us since kindergarten. My post-secondary education has focused on people, behavior, cognition, and cultures. Rod's is in electrical engineering. What does that make us in Haiti? In Haiti, we had to learn how to do laundry by hand. Learn how to handle wild dogs, goats, pigs, tarantulas. How to get coffee. Learn how to survive without electricity, toilets, running water. When we first went down to Haiti, we had to unlearn our own lifestyles and learn basic things. We became children. And it was hilarious to our Haitian friends(kids especially)-- how on earth do these people survive? They can't do anything for themselves! We might have knowledge that is deemed important and powerful in the west-- but survival knowledge? The ability to live without consumerism, technology? If all the world's technology were wiped out, it would be countries like Haiti that survive.

There is so much value and beauty in the knowledge and intelligence that so many Haitians have. We have learned a lot and taken valuable knowledge from the friends we've made in Haiti.

Of course, our work with Haiti doesn't end here. We are in the final stages of getting Medika Mamba to Pignon as a more efficient way to address malnutrition in the smaller villages around Pignon. I can't say that we know what will come next in our plans for Haiti. We have hopes of operating on a larger scale to address needs such as education and malnourishment in villages outside the city. We'll remain devoted and involved with our friends in Pignon, and hope to return in 2013. There are a number of kids on the education program and feeding clinic programs and we will continue to raise money for those more small-scale causes.

Jillayna Adamson

The Other Side of Haiti

Like many countries around the world, Haiti is a nation of many faces. It is many-sided, with its own cultural variances and circumstances brewed within its own different worlds. What much of the remaining world sees or hears about-- be it in desperate flashes across CNN, an article or photograph here and there, or a charity walk-- are a very specific world of Haiti. That of devastation from natural disasters, crime, poverty, corruption. They are the images of crowded tarp tents holding huddles of people after the earthquake, of flooding streets, a ransacked Port Au Prince heated with crime.

I sought to explore and understand the sides of Haiti that may go unnoticed. They too suffer devastation. The little villages, rural scatterings of homes, the tiny towns that you'll cling on the back of someone's beat-up motorbike to get to. They are the quieter areas, the more silent sufferers whose direct battles revolve around health, disease, clean water, schools, hunger, child-trafficking. And yes, many of these areas also felt the pain, the 'aftershocks', of the earthquake, even if they themselves were not directly impacted.

I wrote from a side of Haiti that I have come to love, understand and deeply respect. They suffer, but they smile. They give and love. I was lucky to get to know some of these smaller places, their beautiful, kind, passionate people. Their happy children. Their ways of life. They are places of so little, harbored with endless limitations. But they showed me a deep sense of contentment, joy, and a welcoming without comparison. Haiti is not all about devastation, it is not all tragedy. There are other sides of Haiti so worthy of knowing and understanding. Sometimes they are tucked between mountainsides or hard to find. But they hold an incredible spirit of beautiful people, stories that you won't see on the national news, individuals and circumstances you'll seldom hear of. I can only hope and work toward the belief that they should not be discarded or forgotten. That instead, they are known and celebrated a a part of what Haiti is.

Keep up with us as the journey continues:

Jillayna.blogspot.com

Endless thanks to those who have made donations and encouraged our efforts!

Paul and Deb Adamson

James Adamson

Amy Birse

Ruth and Eric Hoffman

Steve Hurst and Naomi Bartley

Glenda Beecham

David and Laura Karp

Angela Adamson and Cory Baum

Karen and Tom Horn

Kendra and Brian Mcpherson

Mag Bartley

Ken and Edra Adamson

Mike Diamond

Qiqi Liu and Ben

Christy Graves

Randi Howard

Lynne Harman

Kids at the Center for Creative Learning (St. Louis)

Vernell Slack

Penny Nuernberge

Sherryl and Chuck Triplett and kids

Allison Peters

Tom and Connie Peters

Laurel Point Inn, Victoria BC

Barc and Lilly Holbrook

Kathleen Hodges

Sue Cobb

Trish Munson

Bill and Jennifer Campbell

Haiti Outreach

Neil Van Dine

Meds and Food for Kids

Dr.Pat Wolff

David Schwartz

Currently, Jill and Rod hope to develop or become a part of an organization in Pignon and surrounding villages that focuses on feeding clinic efforts and educational support.

To learn more, or make a donation, visit:

Jillayna.blogspot.com

To learn more about Haiti Outreach, visit:

Haitioutreach.org

To learn more about Meds and Food for Kids, visit:

mfkhaiti.org

CPSIA information can be obtained at www.ICGtesting.com
Printed in the USA
BVOW07s1136141214

379329BV00005B/349/P